Our Easter Book

Our Easter Chick

By Jane Belk Moncure
Illustrated by
Mina Gow McLean

THE CHILD'S WORLD
ELGIN, ILLINOIS 60120

Library of Congress Cataloging in Publication Data

Moncure, Jane Belk.
  Our Easter book.

  (A Special Day book)
  SUMMARY: Describes various classroom activities in
preparation for Easter.
  1. Easter—Juvenile literature. 2. Schools—
Exercises and recreations—Juvenile literature.
[1. Easter. 2. Holidays] I. McLean, Mina.
II. Title.
GT4935.M57   372.1´8´9   75-37698
ISBN 0-913778-33-8

Distributed by Childrens Press, 1224 West Van Buren Street,
Chicago, Illinois 60607

This book is about things we did at Easter time in our class. You will have many more ideas in your class.

"Easter time is flower time," said Beth as she handed her teacher a bunch of daffodils.

"Flowers are a lovely sign of spring," said Miss Berry.

"I would like to make some flowers for my friends for Easter," said Beth. She found some muffin cups on the art shelf. "I will make muffin-cup flowers."

Beth cut out paper petals and pasted them around each muffin cup. Then she added green stems and leaves. She put some of the flowers in little pots.

Then Miss Berry showed her how to put her flowers in a basket. First Miss Berry took some of the flowers and pasted them to a paper plate. Then she folded the plate and stapled a handle to it.

Soon there were lovely muffin-cup flowers in Easter baskets all around the room.

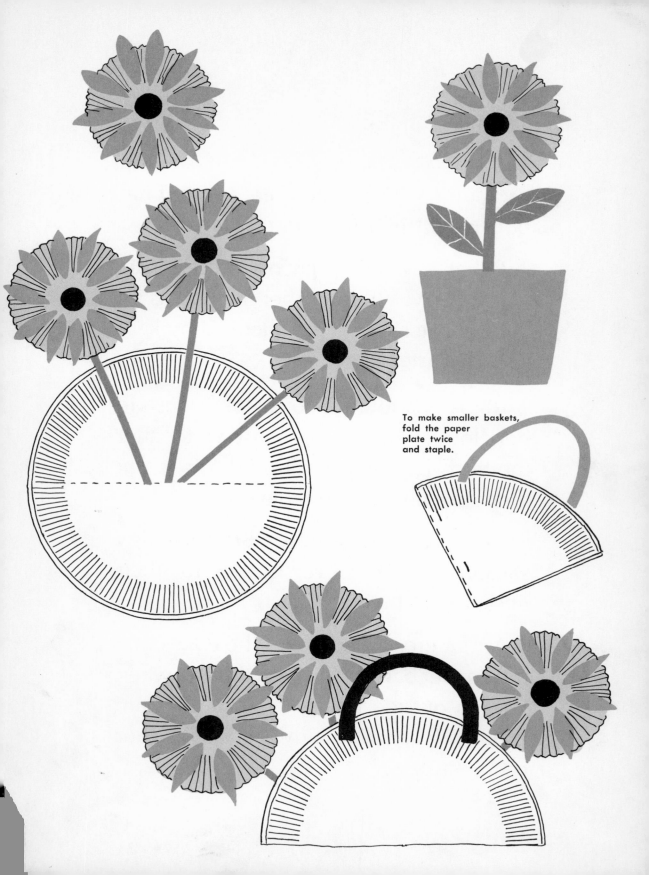

To make smaller baskets,
fold the paper
plate twice
and staple.

"Guess what?" said Kate. "A bird has built a nest in a bush in my yard."

"That is a sure sign of spring," said Miss Berry. "Remember the signs of spring. Later, we'll use them to make a special Easter tree."

Miss Berry found a box of birds' nests in her closet. "I found these last winter after the birds left them," she said as she put them on the science table.

Kate picked up a nest. "Birds use tiny sticks, grass, and even strings for their nest. Could I make a nest?"

Miss Berry rolled down the edges of a little paper bag. "Take this with you when you go outside today," she said. "I am sure you can find tiny sticks for your nest."

Kate filled her bag with sticks and grass. She pasted grass around the outside.

"I need a bird for my nest," she said. "I can draw a bird myself. And I need eggs for my nest. Miss Berry, will you make me some dough?"

Miss Berry mixed a cup of flour with a half cup of salt. She added a little blue water until the mixture was soft but not sticky.

"This is just what I need," said Kate. She rolled the dough into four little blue eggs for her nest. "Now I have an Easter nest."

Jennifer found a caterpillar. She put it in the insect cage.

"Caterpillars are another sign of new life in spring," said Miss Berry.

Miss Berry told the children a story, using a sock-puppet caterpillar and a glove-puppet butterfly.

"This is a caterpillar," she said, "Do you know what happens when he grows fat? One day he makes a chrysalis."

Miss Berry put the caterpillar puppet in a green bag. "I wonder what happens next," she said. She reached her hand into the green bag and pulled out a butterfly puppet.

"He turns into a butterfly," said Jennifer. "That's neat. My caterpillar will do that too."

One day, there was lots of excitement in the room. The eggs in the incubator were hatching.

"One chick is already out of his shell," said Laurie.

"One chick is pecking a little door in his shell so he can come outside," said Meg.

"We will have baby chicks for Easter," said Eddie.

Laurie made a book about the baby chicks. Laurie drew the pictures. Miss Berry wrote the words for her.

Jennifer and Kate made chicken puppets out of paper bags and scraps of yellow paper.

"I am the Easter chick," Jennifer made her puppet say. "Do you know what I do?"

"What?" asked Kate's puppet.

"I make Easter eggs for the Easter bunny!"

The next day was a windy day. "Wind is another sign of spring," said Miss Berry.

"Can we make some kites?" asked David.

"We can make paper kites you can pull in the wind," said Miss Berry. "How many different shapes can you cut?"

There were birds and butterflies and round balloons to pull in the wind. David pasted two triangles together.

"I just made a kite," he said. He drew flowers on it. "An Easter kite," he said.

One day it rained. "Rain is another sign of spring," said Miss Berry.

"Flowers like rain," said Jeff. "It helps them grow."

"Let's dance a story about flowers," said Miss Berry. She played music on her guitar.

"Curl up on the floor, little bulb," chanted Miss Berry. "You are a tulip or a daffodil or an Easter lily bulb. You are down under the ground. The rain rains above you. Now the sun shines. What do you do?"

"We grow," said Jeff.

Slowly the children grew taller and taller, then stood there swaying in the breeze.

"You have grown into flowers," sang Miss Berry. "Dance, flowers, dance."

After music time, Miss Berry said, "I have some seeds in this box. We found them last fall in something orange. Who remembers?"

"Our pumpkin seeds! Our pumpkin seeds!" Everyone remembered.

"I saved them," said Miss Berry, "so we could grow pumpkin plants for Easter."

Miss Berry gave each child a cup, a spoon, and two pumpkin seeds. She put a can of rich brown earth in the center of each table.

"I will give my mother a pumpkin plant for Easter," said Jeff.

The days were getting warmer.

"Today we are going to help decorate our Easter tree in the hall," said Miss Berry. "Every year we make new things for the Easter tree. Make something you have seen this spring."

Children made flowers, eggs, nests, butterflies, birds, tadpoles, rain drops, and sunshine circles to hang on the tree.

Kate hung a lovely blue feather she found in her yard.

It was time to dye Easter eggs. Each person brought a hard-boiled egg to school.

Miss Berry put newspapers on the tables. Then she put cups of Easter egg dye around each table.

After all the eggs were colored, Miss Berry gave each person a handful of white cotton balls.

"Touch a cotton ball in each color and see what happens," she said.

"I have a blue egg and rainbow colored cotton balls," said Meg.

It was time to talk about the Easter surprise. "Easter time is a time when the world is full of new life," said Miss Berry. "You have seen new flowers, baby chicks..."

"...and birds," said Kate.

"...and caterpillars," said Jennifer.

"Friday," continued Miss Berry, "we are going to see more baby animals. We are going to the petting zoo."

Everybody thought that was a great idea. The children took messages home, stapled to the backs of little bunny puppets.

When the children walked inside the petting zoo, Miss Berry gave each child an ice cream cone filled with cracked corn.

"This is an Easter basket for the animals," she said. The children fed baby goats, lambs, and a little calf, and chicks. Two little deer followed them all around. There were many other baby animals to pet and hold.

When it was time to go, Miss Berry gave each child an empty ice cream cone. "On your way to the cars, you may find candy Easter eggs to put in your Easter baskets," she said.

"Who ever heard of an ice cream cone Easter basket?" asked Jeff. He picked up a candy Easter egg. "I can eat my egg and my basket too."

E
~~379.1~~
MON

76-765

Moncure, Jane Belk

Our Easter book